From Where I Stand

Charleston, SC
www.PalmettoPublishing.com

From Where I Stand
Copyright © 2022 by Joyce Ann Key

Hardcover ISBN: 979-8-8229-0920-5
Paperback ISBN: 979-8-8229-0921-2
eBook ISBN: 979-8-8229-0922-9

From Where I Stand

MEMOIRS of a HAIRSTYLIST

JOYCE ANN KEY

Dedication

To the memory of my moma, Wilma Cook

Table of Contents

Foreword

I believe there are only a handful of people in each person's life who rank as truly special. And I can honestly say that Wilma Cook makes my very exclusive list. When I hear her name, I still smile—every time. And that's because I can still remember her playful voice greeting me on Sunday afternoons when we gathered after church for her famous pot roast. I can remember the many Thanksgivings that she and I would make a mincemeat pie together; she and I would say we were the only ones who liked it. But as funny and witty as she was, she was more caring. She could take you by the hand and tell you anything; you never knew what Wilma was going to say. Everyone who knew her knew that! But whatever it was, it was said with love. I'm grateful I was chosen to write the foreword. And it's my way of saying just one more time, "I love you, Wilma." Joyce Ann has done a magnificent job of capturing the Wilma I knew. I truly loved this book from cover to cover, and I believe you will too.

—Jeff Curry

Introduction

I do not plan on this memoir being long because I do not want anyone who reads this to be bored by my stories; I want them to be inspired, touched, and a little amused by them. Just thinking about my moma's humble country beginnings, her short education but the great impact her life behind the chair had on so many beckons the stories. Many cannot be told, but I have shared the ones that can be. The lessons I learned from watching, the reflections of growing up in simpler times, and the one thing that has not changed as a hairstylist in an industry that is always evolving—human connection.

Beginnings

I know I did not go into this career with an end in mind. It is for sure my moma (pronounced mama but she spelled it with an "o") did not either! Truthfully, at the age I received my cosmetology license, twenty, I did not even think of the beginning. To me, my mom always was, as she put it, a "beauty operator." Nowadays, we, or most of us, prefer to be called a hairstylist. It was what I grew accustomed to and what I related to because my mom spent a lot of time at the salon, and therefore I did too. I have been wanting to tell a few of her stories and my perception of them for a long time while my memory serves me well and so my mom, now ninety-three, can read it and share her thoughts.

I do not know if anyone will care, maybe not, but every time I tell a story, especially of moms, I hear the words that encourage me to do this! "Joyce, you have got to write a book about her." So here it goes; I hope it is enjoyable, encouraging, and insightful on this wonderful and fulfilling career of mine and Wilma Cook's. Also, I hope it is encouraging to anyone who might be feeling like they are not smart, pretty, or educated enough to be or have a career in something, especially hairstyling. You are always a work in progress. After thirty-eight years in an ever-changing industry, I can say I am still learning and hopefully getting better. The requirements are willingness and fortitude. Also, a love of people because you will meet all kinds and must adjust. Really, it is my mother's story that I have been blessed to have a front-row seat in. I will always cherish the memories, and I want to share them! Someday, maybe I just might write about more of my own. But for now, my stories behind the chair are still being written.

Sidelined

Since starting this memoir, I have had a huge life update.

Sadly, as I write this, I have been derailed. To my complete heartbreak, my iconic "Beauty Operator" mom fell suddenly ill in November of 2018, and she passed away on November 14, 2018! Not only do I miss her, I now feel like it is my call to complete this book. She knew I was writing a memoir, and somehow, I will complete it in honor of my mom; hopefully it will bring some comfort to me. I set this aside for years, not thinking I would ever pick it back up. I am thankful to share her through my eyes.

Destiny

I guess I was destined to do hair. From the time I can remember, my life has always revolved around a beauty shop! Now a beauty shop is called a salon—sounds fancier but it is what it is. I guess like everything else, it truly is a bit fancier, with Pinterest and other inspiring websites that have brought out the decorators in us, and we now have some beautiful spaces to "do hair" these days! Being a hairstylist is so much more than a finished look. I want to convey that through this writing. It is the time spent listening to your client and styling their hair, but it is also a connection between you and your client. Obviously, you need to have a bend toward hairstyling, and naturally for me, I do by genetics and because I have been around it all my life.

I tried once to step into another career right after I married and we moved to Sherman, Texas, just because the thought of trying to start building a clientele again was too daunting. So I applied to become a sales rep for Paul Mitchell hair products. I did get hired and trained, but it only lasted a month—talk about a square peg in a round hole. It goes without saying that I did not fit. I just missed standing behind the chair and went right back to hairdressing as fast as I could! My mom, however, never would give up on it even till the end. The craft and people just get in your blood.

Places, Sights, and Sounds

The landscape of salons has certainly changed. The good ol' days were all open concept: your chair was part of a row of others; even the shampoo areas had different chairs and overall looks back in the day. I know there are still a few like these in places, but most seasoned stylists now work in a more private setting—salon suites.

I know if that had been the thing back when my mom or even when I started, these stories would not be told because they would not have been witnessed, at least by me. I work in a suite and love the privacy, but I feel very fortunate to have had the experiences of the openness my mom had her entire career, spanning sixty-plus years. That is not the only thing that has changed in the salon world; everything has gone ecofriendly, smoke-free, paraben-free, sulfate-free, and so on. I know that is better in every way, but my younger days included these and even hair spray smelled and worked better back then! Moma always came home smelling like the beauty shop, a little bit of a combination of hair spray and perm. No one had any inkling in those days that the fumes were bad. Ignorance was bliss, but those beehive hairdos would hold up through a tornado! The brush rollers she used, the perms, metal teasing combs, just to name a few, have been replaced or upgraded.

I remember summer days hanging out in the beauty shop. Old fashioned Coke machines filled with bottles of ice-cold Coca Cola, Fresca, and Tab! I would stay all day; my bare feet were coated with hair spray and hair! You might think that sounds disgusting, but for me, it was awesome and meant I had spent a day at my home away from home—the beauty shop!

I always had the best time seeing all her customers too. One of the salons she worked at, the owner had two daughters—Jill and Jan. We would play with our Barbies in another room while our moms were fixing hair; it was fun. We might get told to clean the hair out of brush rollers or restock the Coke box or empty ashtrays.

Sometimes we walked across the street to the diner and got milkshakes or lunch. I really do not think I ever got bored or minded going to work with Mom.

The Poly Salon; Aunt Margaret

Before the Chair
and Surprises

Mom was originally a stay-at-home mom to my brothers, Welton and Roger. I am seventeen years younger than my oldest brother Welton. I cannot even imagine her not working; it is hard for me to picture her in that role. However, she suffered from anxiety disorder, and she needed an outlet of some sort. Mom said she had inherited this from my grandmother. Anxiety and panic attacks are no joke and can really get the best of you. The doctor advised Mom to get a hobby or a job to try to redirect her mind, and it helped her tremendously.

My brothers said she decided to go to beauty school at night with her friend Patsy. Patsy and her family were neighbors and close friends among the tight knit community where they lived in the Poly suburb of Fort Worth,

Texas. My brother said she went to school after she would get supper ready and washed and pressed their clothes for the next school day. Being good at styling hair and a very caring and service-oriented person, she became a hairstylist and got her cosmetology license when my brothers were old enough to be more independent. Cosmetology school proved to be a good fit for her, and she was naturally great at it, but then she was great at everything. Perhaps she was not great at traveling; she preferred being home, but styling hair and helping people, she had down to perfection! Wish I could ask what my dad thought, but I never did. As I can recall, he never seemed to mind.

My daddy was a quiet, hardworking family man and an electrician by trade. He was a World War II veteran, loved playing golf, and loved his family. He and Mom were very traditional in the makeup of the family back in those days. Her going to work must have been an adjustment. I know it gave them a little extra income but also know it gave her so much more in relationships and an outlet to use her giftings of hairstyling and serving others.

Just a few years into her hairdressing days, she was not feeling good. Thinking she was getting sick; she went back to see the doctor. My oldest brother Welton drove her as Dad was working. To her and everyone's complete surprise and mom's embarrassment, she was going to have another child. Back then, you did not even say "pregnant;" it was a word considered risqué in the sixties. Also, it was a shock and miracle as she had only one ovary and was advanced in age. You could not test anyone back then or do sonograms to know a gender. My maternal grandparents were encouraging, saying that they prayed she would have a girl. My brothers were in high school; my oldest brother Welton was a senior. I was told that he took it better than my other brother, Roger. Roger did not want to discuss it at all, and he did not even want to know my name until a week after I was born. He did come around and accept me along with everyone else. I was the only girl on the block!

Well, the rest is history, but she had given birth to her protégé—me, ha.

Staying home with me was never a thought. She had found her niche, and it worked for her in every way. Her customers were elated, she said, and could not wait for her to bring me to the beauty shop, and she could not either. She had become attached to so many of them and wanted to take her new baby to meet them.

So, when I say I have known a salon all my life, I have, as well as a lot of my mom's customers. I can remember way over a dozen of them: some of her coworkers and even some of their stories. Like my mom, I have gotten attached to many of my own customers over the years and feel like they are extensions of my family. Truly, many leave a lasting mark on your heart.

The only girl on the block

Daddy and my brothers

Suella

The very first memory I have is riding to work with Mom and stopping by on the way to pick up her assistant, Suella! Oh, Suella, there are simply no words to describe her, but she was amazing! I thought I was related to her, and her skin color did not give me any clue that I was not. She was beautiful inside and out and so kind to me! Mom told of me crying one day because I was not the same color as Suella; I wanted to look just like her. She had to explain to me that God made us all different. Moma, I, and everyone loved her.

She was kind, friendly, beautiful, and excellent at what she did. She was mom's best friend, confidant, side-kick, and shampoo assistant for at least thirty years! She could read mom's mind and knew exactly what she needed. Like when to rinse the perm or color off, which customer was next, and every other detail…she knew it all. I remember her washing my hair and using this amazing creme rinse called One Step by Avon. It would make my long hair feel like silk, and Suella's magic touch could get all my tangles out without any pain! I do not know if she knew it or not, but I idolized her! Even as I grew up, married, and moved away, Suella was special to me!

Suella

Moma and Suella

Beauty School Days

Having been raised and rooted in a salon, it is no surprise that I wanted to follow in my moma's footsteps and go to beauty school after I finished high school. I started talking about it before graduation, wanting to start at Ogle School of Hair Design in Hurst, Texas in the Fall of 1982.

Moma however was against it! She told me she wanted me to go to college at the local junior college and after a year if I did not like it, she would pay my entire tuition at Ogle. It sounded like a good plan, and though I had no intention of doing anything other than hair, I took her up on the offer. Truthfully, I know she and my daddy would have paid my tuition to Ogle even if I had insisted on going right away, but by waiting a year, I could start at the same time as one of my best friends, Shari, who also planned on going to Ogle's but was a year behind me in graduating high school. Also, I could attend junior college with another one of my best friends, Brenda. So waiting was a win-win for me!

If it surprises anyone that Moma did not want me to choose hairdressing as my profession, truthfully it did me too until lately. I realize now that when I asked and she said she didn't want me to, she was the same age as I am now—fifty-eight. I'm sure she was feeling the effects in her hands, legs, feet, and back of standing eight–twelve hours on any given day. Along with no monetary benefits such as health insurance and 401(k). All I saw at my age then was the relationships and gratification of not only making people feel pretty but interacting with them and helping them feel encouraged. But now I understand why she had the hope that I would pursue something else, as I have the same aches and pains, but I would not change a thing, and I know she wouldn't either!

In a Nutshell

When I first became a hairstylist, I got to work with Moma and Suella at The Nut Shell Boutique and Beauty Shop! It was fun to be their coworker and not the kid that just hung out at the beauty shop. Suella and I bonded even more over cooking and recipes! We would cut them out of *Southern Living* and *Taste of Home* magazines or write them on recipe cards. No internet, Google, or Pinterest back then!

The Nut Shell was also a boutique, so often Suella would give me her opinion on the latest outfit I would try on. They would put outfits in the back of the boutique that they wanted me to try on and thought I would look good in, and usually I would like them. Of course, I loved working where there were cute clothes! It was, however, more suited to ladies older than me, but I liked some of the clothes. Moma would also love helping her customers find a great blouse or jacket in the boutique while their hair was being processed or their hair was drying.

Sometimes, I worked in the boutique on Mondays. It was a great segue to begin my hairstyling career there as I was very comfortable in the environment. The owners and store manager were wonderful. Those ladies, Mom, and Suella were so much fun. It was enjoyable and enlightening hanging out with all of them! I look back, and I think it significantly helped me in a positive way to be influenced by them all.

The owner, Nell, had this unmistakable laugh! She was stick skinny, vivacious, and a spitfire. She and her family were the kindest people and had a ranch somewhere outside of the DFW area. I just remember she talked about going there a lot.

The store manager Nini was the opposite of Nell in looks and personality. She was dramatic and had the appearance of refinement. Her hair was usually in a French twist, and she had this fair, dewy skin. I believe she had been an opera singer back in her younger days, so you can imagine the contrast between her and the owner.

Then there was another lady who worked there who was somewhere in the middle, Billie; she had a Southern charm about her. Classy and stylish but also very warm. I loved them all, and Mom did too. Every Christmas they would decorate the boutique and serve hot cider out of a metal percolator. It is all vivid to me, such a special, fun, and simpler time.

There were a few stylists who came and left besides Mom in those Nut Shell days. One being Sheila, a beautiful redhead with a sexy voice. Mom loved her and would often describe her as that pretty redhead! Sheila and I even worked together years later at a different salon. I remember another coworker of Mom's worked at a bar at night. She would rinse hair with beer, as Mom told me, saying it gave hair more volume! Mom worked at The Nut Shell until it closed, but she stayed in the same shopping center, working at two other salons that moved in there until she was forced to stop at ninety-one years of age due to her back. This was long after most of her peers had stopped working, passed away, or moved.

(sitting) Nel Bannister, owner with her husband, Wm. L, Billie Kohen, Left to right, standing.Pati Alexander, Joyce Cook, Wilma Cook, Jennifer Crabtree, and Suella Young.

Newspaper clipping from the Nut Shell days

Wilma (Moma) Cook

Joyce Cook Key

Wilma and Joyce Ann

Wilma (Moma) and Suella at the Nutshell

Shopping Bag from the Nutshell

Granny and Poly

Mom and Suella did not start out at that shopping center; however, they started out in the Poly area of Fort Worth.

There she worked with many ladies whom I can recall. Suella, of course, Margie, and Margaret from way back stand out to me. Mom did a lady named Bessie Tidwell's hair at that time; she also did two of her daughters' hair too.

When Mom had me, she had to bring me to the beauty shop with her. I was only three weeks old. She could not take off any longer, and my grandmother lived too far away to keep me. So back to the salon she went, with me in tow. I can only imagine, but I have been told that I was passed around and held by all her customers.

That is when Bessie, whom we called Granny Tidwell, offered to keep me. Mom loved her, and soon she started watching me every Tuesday through Friday. Moma would drop me off, and my daddy picked me up around

5:00 p.m. Right before he would get there, she'd have me sit on the floor and brush my long hair to have me ready to go home; I loved it. She always cooked really well and would always make us hot lunches every day. That is where I first ate squash. I just adored Granny so much; she really was like a grandma to me, and she treated me so well. Granny kept me for many years, and even after I grew up enough to stay by myself, I kept in touch. Granny also kept her grandkids, and it was like I was one of them.

Granny's daughter Barbara was also like family. She took me everywhere with her kids and Granny. Barbara even took me to see Elvis in concert when I was about ten years old. I will never forget that. I guess that is what began my love of Elvis and his music! To this day, I am a fan!

Granny, Barbara, and her kids were usually even at my birthday parties.

Granny "Bessie" Tidwell

Barbara

Wigs and Me

Staying with Granny kept me out of Mom's hair at the salon, literally.

When I was three or four, she had me at the beauty shop one day. She was fixing one of her ladies' hairs, but she had left her wig for Mom to style and told mom she would pick it up later. Many of her customers did that as back in the sixties and seventies it was commonplace to wear wig or wiglets. That day, she had me with her at the beauty shop but I disappeared, and then she found me in the back room cutting this lady's wig. She said, "Oh no, Joyce Ann, what are you doing?" I responded and told her "It is ok, Wilma. (I called her that when I was little.) I am just shortening the long!" I called her Wilma as that is what I would hear all the time being around older people. I guess I can say that was my first haircut, and Mom said it was actually pretty good!

Thelma Jo and Rolls

One thing is for sure, political correctness was not a part of Mom's personality! She had this unique way of telling her opinion and still everyone loved her! She was brutally honest about what she thought and how it affected her or anyone she cared for! Still her honest and sincere charm was received most of the time without much fallout!

One of my funniest memories of this occurred after I had started doing hair myself. I was straight out of beauty school, working at The Nut Shell with Moma and Suella. It was a busy Saturday for Mom, and one of her dearest customers Thelma Jo Corn was drying her roller-set hair under the dryer. Mom had a terrible headache that day, and Thelma Jo was notorious for singing while her hair dried. As usual, she began singing, and Mom, already working on the next customer, set her comb down and walked over to Thelma, raised her dryer, and told Thelma she had to shut that singing up and be quiet because her head was killing her and she just could not stand it! Thelma never made another sound, but I was mortified! Suella, looked through the cut out in the wall, and we both looked like our eyes would pop out of our heads!

I said, "Mom, that was rude!"

She said "Joyce Ann, Thelma knows I do not mean anything by it, but I cannot stand any noise today!"

She was right; I believe Thelma hugged and kissed Mom on the cheek, telling her, "Darling, feel better!" She was back the next week, and all was well!

Moma could not only fix hair, but she was the best at helping everyone! She was always giving; it was just her way! Several of her ladies could barely afford to live on their social security. She charged them only a few dollars, if anything. I distinctly remember one lady in particular, Mrs. Lee.

She would make homemade rolls every Saturday! After Mom got home on Saturdays and changed out of her salon-smelling clothes and freshened her makeup, she, Dad, and I would go out to eat. On the way, we had to stop over to pick up our rolls from Mrs. Lee! She would have a dozen ready, piping hot, and they smelled delicious! We would have them for lunch on Sundays if we did not devour them beforehand. This was how she paid mom for her hair, and looking back, I know Moma had to adore her and the hot rolls to accept that week after week. Still her generous heart was ok with it, and my daddy did not seem to mind driving over there to pick them up either. There were others over the years; some she just barely charged as she could not bear for them not to have a hairdo for church on Sunday.

Death Has a Smell

My parents and I attended a local Baptist church. It was small and one of many in our city, but we loved it. Moma had lots of customers from there, and she loved being their hairdresser and friend.

One day after one of the older men had come in for his monthly haircut, Moma looked at Suella with concern and said, "You know what Suella? He smelled funny to me." Suella asked her what she meant, and Moma explained that she thought he smelled like he was going to die. Moma said there is a look and a smell people have; I do not know what exactly that is, but she just always told me that.

Anyway, within a few days, she got a call while she was working that he had passed away. He had been having some health issues. When Mom told Suella the news, she said, "Wilma, don't be smelling me!" I guess you can say she had lots of discernment. I know they were both sad at the news. She told my daddy when she got home the story. I just recall my daddy saying, "Oh, Wilma!" a lot. She was always saying, "I have a funny feeling…"

Connections and Disconnections

When I learned to use the phone, it was my daily need to hear my mom's voice while she was working. When I was old enough to stay by myself, I was the latchkey kid. After school, she always wanted me to call and let her know I got home. During the summer, however, I think I drove her crazy calling the salon to ask when she would be home, if I could go over to a friend's house, or what we were going to have for dinner.

Before cell phones or even cordless phones, my calls were more annoying to the receptionist than to Moma! She would have to leave her workstation and go to the desk to get the phone call. This annoys me just telling it, but anyway, I started using her customers' names to try and trick the receptionist into thinking it was someone besides me again calling my mom so much! I was stuck saying, "Is Wilma there? It's Ms. Gandy," one of her favorite customers. If you have ever heard my voice, it is pretty telling! I am sure they all laughed at my attempt to disguise myself, even if I was a nuisance!

After I started doing hair, I continued calling Moma every morning and evening before and after work from my cell phone in the car! I cherish those short conversations on my drive to and from work! Sometimes she would not even say hello but just answer and say, "You on your way?" I miss those daily briefings of our day to each other! Mom was always so funny! At the end of the day when I call, she would always say, "Why are you so late getting off" or "How'd you do?" I would love to hear her tell me what she saw on *Dr. Phil* or what she had done all day. She would also give me a daily news report and just have the funniest spin on things. One thing you did not want to do is call her when she was watching her favorite soap opera, *Days of Our Lives*. She would rush you off the phone. It is those little things you miss.

Cutting the Cord

I only worked with her for a brief time.

I decided I needed to cut the cord and with her encouragement went down the road to work with a popular male stylist James. Mom encouraged me; she wanted me to be exposed to more current trends in hair and felt like I would be held back working with "all us old ladies" as she put it. I also think I may have been a little bored, and she knew it. As I have grown up though, I understand you just can't be around your mom 24-7 when you're a young adult. I do not care how much you love each other. So, I went about a mile down the road to work at a more "modern" salon as she would put it.

It was a great move for me, and I did learn a lot from the many trendsetting stylists there. Maybe also some things my moma would not want me to know, and I am not talking about hair. I even went to a hair show in New

Orleans with them. So, I am sure you can imagine how much fun that was at the ripe age of twenty-one!

Working there was enlightening in every way, and I grew more confident in my skills, working with the infamous James. He had a prestigious clientele too, and I even met a former Miss Texas beauty contestant. Back then, James was one of the top stylists in the area. His hairstyling skills were impressive. I remember sitting on a stool by him, watching as he combed out hair; it was like watching an artist. Not to mention, I really was there to talk to him and his customers. I developed a relationship with them, and James threw me a wedding shower and invited them; it was wonderful. Moma's customers did as well; it was such a blessing for Russell and me.

My mom was so pleased to know I was there, working and learning from James. I think one of her many attributes was that she always was proud of other stylists' successes and truly admired not just me but just about everyone she knew in this industry. She would say, "Joyce Ann, no one can do hair like James!" Or "If you want to have beautiful red-colored hair, go see Sheila!" Or "Let us make an appointment, and let Doreen cut your hair." Doreen was also a well-known stylist in the area, and back then, everyone was getting the Farrah cut! We all wanted that look, and I had found out a popular girl in my high school with the best Farrah cut went to Doreen. I just wanted that hair so bad, so Mom made an appointment for me. The things we do for our kids, but to no avail; my hair did not quite look like I had pictured it. This was not due to the haircut; not everyone's hair comes out the same.

Relentless

My mom's claim to fame was she could roll a perm on any head of hair in a New York minute; she was fast. She also could do some great teasing! Also, her work ethic and dedication were bar none, better than anyone I have ever seen to this day.

It even made me mad at times. She would often go to work sick, and an ambulance was called a couple of times. This was later in her life; she was around eighty-five. I would be called; we had moved back to the DFW area, and I was working in a salon in Hurst, Texas. I would be frantic and leave my customer to go see what was wrong with her at a nearby hospital emergency room. Thankfully, one time it was a bad UTI; the other time it was vertigo. She would say, "Joyce Ann, honey, I am sorry. I just all of a sudden got so weak...you did not need to come." Oh, but yes, I did. Then, the next day she would head right back down to that beauty shop.

At that time, Sheila was working with me at another salon. Many of us working there had bought these stylish smocks to wear over our clothes while doing hair. The zipper was blingy, and I told Sheila I was going to buy my moma one for her upcoming birthday, September 11. Sheila encouraged me to and said it can be her shroud! She knew Mom well and that she would work till she could not stand anymore or just die behind that chair.

Keeping It Real and Positive

As much as I worried, got frustrated, or became mad, I would not stay mad long. Mom would be the first one I would call during my lowest times as a stylist. Rejection is never fun, and I admittedly take it hard. One lady I had been seeing every Friday for several years asked me to sit down after I finished styling her hair one Friday. She then informed me that she loved my "hairdoing" and she thought I was great, but she was leaving me to go back to her former stylist in Grapevine, Texas. She then said the Lord was telling her to do so! I was so shocked, hurt, and asked, "Are you sure I did not do anything to upset or offend you?" I could not imagine what it would have been, but thought I would ask anyway.

She said "Oh no, you have done nothing wrong." I was so upset; I went to my car and called my moma. I told her what happened and what the lady had said about the Lord telling her to go see another stylist in Grapevine.

My moma listened and then said, "Joyce Ann, the good Lord does not care about where that old lady gets her hair done, and furthermore, you don't either."

I said, "I don't?"

She said, "No, you don't; just forget it, and focus on the ones you've got in that beauty shop right now. Stop crying; I have been through that." She then said, "Mark my words, she will call back one day, and you might be too busy to take her, but if you do, she'll do it again."

A year later, the lady called asking me to please do her hair again. I took her back, and just like my moma said, after a year or so, she did do it again. In a slightly different way but lesson learned.

I think I might have toughened up a little. It still hurt though.

Only four months before Moma passed, I called her another time, crying. I had just learned of the passing of one of my older ladies and dearest customers. I was sobbing from the laundry room in my current salon. I saw this customer every Friday.

Moma said, "Joyce Ann, I have been through that a zillion times; it is awful, but be thankful you had the time you had with her. She is better off."

I kept crying, and she asked me again, "Aren't you thankful you had time with her?"

"Yes," I said. She just put a positive spin on everything.

When Moma passed, I told one of my friends what she would be saying about it. "Well, that Wilma, she's better off." She would laugh that I would say that, imitating her. But in reality, because of her faith, she is.

Selfless

I was thinking about something she told me she had to help one of her customers with at work! She had to clean up a lady in the restroom and wash her clothes after the poor lady had an accident soiling her pants. I was amazed as I listened to her, and I said "Moma, I don't know how you can do some of the things you do!" She was well into her eighties.

She said, "Joyce Ann, when I was younger, I was really sick, and I asked the good Lord to help me and promised him I'd be good to people all my life!" When I think of all she has done to help everyone I know, I want to cry! She had more wisdom than some I know with a PhD, compassion, humility, and an abundance of grace, dignity, and love! I hope someday I can be like her!

Knowing that God gave her the strength and desire to help others still just blesses my heart. Well into her eighties and after she had worked all day at the salon, she would drive over to cut the hair of one of her elderly male customers who was blind and could not drive to the salon anymore for his haircuts. She would also make many trips to the nursing homes to help make some of her customers feel better by fixing their hair. She was always trying to help someone.

Looking Good

If you need a life coach, counselor, personal assistant, style consultant, or friend, look no further than your hairstylist. My mom was the best of these! She was always looking out for her customers and cared deeply for them till the end!

One time, one of her favorite ladies was in for her weekly hairdo and arrived looking "just awful" according to Mom! She had been working in the yard and had not showered, changed clothes, or put on any makeup as she normally would have before her hair appointment. The problem was mom had received word from the lady's family earlier that week that they were going to pick her up after the hair appointment to surprise her for a birthday dinner. So, when she walked in, Mom told her, "Dorothy, you better run back to the house and change clothes and put on a little makeup, honey! Your kids are coming here to surprise you for dinner!"

"Oh, damn, Wilma!" she proclaimed! She then went home to spruce up, and her family were unaware that mom had told her! Dorothy was so grateful, and Moma thought it was funny, but she was proud she had saved Dorothy the embarrassment! Years later when Dorothy passed away, Moma told her family what happened that day, and they laughed at the fun memory. Mom said she could not bear Dorothy not looking her best for the fun celebration that awaited her! Thank goodness Mom told her; I am sure she acted surprised and looked great!

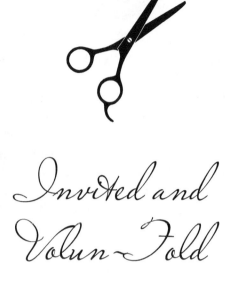

Invited and Volun-Told

Not long after Russell and I had moved to Sherman, Texas, I was doing hair at JCPenney in the salon at the mall. I had very few "regular clients;" most were call-ins, but I did manage to retain a few. Being marginally decent at teasing hair, most of the ones who were standing customers of mine were about twenty–forty years older than I was. I was only around twenty-eight or twenty-nine years old.

A very nice and wealthy customer of mine brought me an invitation one day to the salon. She invited me to come to a luncheon at her home. To say I was excited was an understatement. If you know me, you know I love social gatherings, and I felt honored and special to be included. I arrived at the designated time, dressed in my best outfit at her lovely home. I was a little surprised that there were only a couple of other cars there. When she opened the door and invited me in, she was happy to see me and showed me where to set my purse. Then she asked if I would mind, but she needed a few extra hands getting the house ready. I said, "Sure, of course." Then she handed me a dust cloth and showed me where to clean. I then realized that she just needed me to help her get things ready for her "real guests," making me feel second class.

After I left that day, I could not wait to call my mom and tell her what went down and how it made me feel. She listened and said, "Joyce Ann, she just knew she could count on you, honey, and you are ok! You enjoyed it, didn't you? I know you do not like just sitting around, and I know she appreciated you, so let it go!" She was right, I did!

Sprucing Up

Moma truly wanted people to feel good about them-
selves inwardly and outwardly, and she wanted them to
look pretty or handsome. I think she saw a correlation.
It was sometimes too much as she would volunteer me
to help her with those things! Anytime someone in the
family needed a little sprucing up with their hair, she
would go get the stool out of the garage and insist upon
me cutting their hair! I admittedly did not always enjoy
that on Sunday afternoons, but it would happen anyway.
She would say, "Listen, Joyce Ann, you have to!"

Sometimes on Mondays, before we would leave for
shopping, I would walk into her house and she would be
standing there wet headed. She would say, "Honey, you
have to fix my hair today; I look awful."

Sunday haircuts

Heaven Ready

Before my moma passed from this earth, she had been in the hospital for two weeks. She was not aware for most of that time, but her hair was not looking to good. I would have fixed it, but it was not possible. When she passed, I asked my friend Shari to fix her hair for the funeral. Unfortunately, her schedule and the time of availability with the funeral home did not coincide, so I told the funeral home to just use their stylist and left them a picture of how Moma wore her hair. I just could not do it myself; it was too hard for me. I went by to preview her before the visitation in the afternoon. Moma's hair was washed and blow-dried and looked clean but not as full and fluffy as she normally wore it. I just thought, "Well, I really can't do anything about it now."

The evening of her visitation, my friends all came for support. Shari walked by me hurriedly with a curling iron and hair spray in her hand! I went back into the parlor where my mother lay, and there was Shari along with another good friend and hairstylist Tracy setting up the makeshift funeral-home salon. I said, "What are y'all doing?" Tracy proclaimed, "Joyce, we can't send Wilma Cook to heaven with her hair that flat!" Shari and Tracy began curling and teasing, and Moma did look 100 percent better! I know she was smiling down, so thank you friends! The troops rallied in my hour of need and support; we even took a picture.

Miracles

Now for miracles…I must share the most life-changing event that came through my time and Mom's from her career. I'm positive she didn't expect that through her hairdressing relationship, Russell and I would become parents! Russell and I had been transferred to Tyler, Texas, by his company. Mom was still working at the Nut Shell.

Early one morning, we were talking on the phone, and she said, "Joyce Ann, I had the funniest dream." I asked what? She said, "I dreamed I got you a baby." Russell and I had been trying to conceive for a couple of years. If she had a dream about a baby for us, I know she'd been thinking about it too. There is no telling how many prayers she, Suella, and her customer Fern had prayed on behalf of Russell and me.

Then out of the blue, Barbara came to the salon one day and asked Mom if Russell and I might consider adoption. That evening, Mom called me and said, "Joyce Ann, listen to me. Barbara came to see me today; she asked me a very important question, and I told her yes!" I asked what? She said, "Barbara asked if you and Russell would adopt a baby; if so, she knows someone who is pregnant but is going to have to put the baby up for adoption." I just about fell out of my chair and really thought no way! No way could it work out for us; nothing ever seemed to. She went on to say, "Barbara is going to call you. I gave her your number!"

I said, "Mom, that is nice, but I don't think it's that easy."

She said, "Listen, Joyce Ann, Barbara wouldn't tell me this for nothing; you wait and see. She will call you." And she did. The miracle happened, and we became parents a few short months later! I had prayed for years to be a mom, for Russell and I to be parents. I never expected that it would be this way. I had my thoughts in a box, a small box. It blew my mind that it could or would happen this way! God is boundless in capabilities and had a plan for us all! Thankful for a faith-filled Moma who didn't give up praying for us!

Adoption is wonderful, and we are blessed with two children because of it. This miracle certainly opened my heart to seeing and thinking outside the box. I still marvel at this story to this day! Just realize this: every relationship or circumstance you have could be the door God uses to lead you to a miracle!

When our son Erik was two, we had gone out to dinner to celebrate the second anniversary of his adoption finalization day. When we arrived home, we had a blinking light on our answering machine that indicated a message had been left for us. I listened while Russell was bringing Erik in and getting him in his pj's for the night. It was our adoption attorney. He left a message to call him; he had something to discuss with us. It was late, and still, I tried to call that evening. Of course, no one answered, and I had to leave a message. I worried all night, thinking the worst possible scenarios; Russell, however, said maybe he was just calling to say, "Happy Finalization Day." I, however, couldn't imagine why the call would have happened on the anniversary if it didn't have something to do with Erik.

The next morning, as soon as I thought the office would open, I called. He wasn't available, and I left him another message. I called my moma and rallied the troops to pray for whatever the message was going to be. He finally called, and it was not at all what I thought. He wanted to ask us if we would consider another adoption. I was speechless, and he had no clue it was Erik's adoption anniversary when he had called. When I mentioned that it had been and my concern, he said, "Oh, that's cool, but I really didn't realize that." He went on to say he was calling on behalf of another family who had reached out to him to ask us. I called Russell immediately to tell him. He didn't hesitate upon realizing the significance of the day and just said, "Well, it's a confirmation from God that this is from him." The rest is history and private, but God knows.

However, in less than two months of that call, we had another miracle—Ethan arrived. We are so thankful for the blessings of our sons through adoption and for their birth moms.

Seven months after the birth of our second son, Ethan, I began feeling off. Everything tasted weird, and I felt extremely tired. My friend Shari and I were working together at a salon, and I told her; she insisted I was pregnant. I told her, "No, I just have a virus or something."

She said, "No, you don't; I think you're pregnant, and I'm buying the test." She did buy me a test and insisted I take it right after work. So, I did, and it was positive. My teeth almost fell out of my head; it was completely unexpected. Here I was with two little miracles and completely content with our family of four. But God had other plans and brought yet another son, Evan, into the fold.

In year two of his life, we began seeing some oddities in his behavior. Besides just a mother's intuition, I also had two children now to compare him to, and it wasn't adding up. Evan was diagnosed with autism, a neurological disorder.

I don't have a doubt that I would have had a complete nervous breakdown if it wasn't for my moma and her prayers those days. She encouraged us, loved us, supported us, and, on one or more occasions, even said, "Joyce, maybe he's normal and we aren't." She was referring to the sweet and loving nature of most children with disorders. All children, the planned and unplanned, are gifts from God.

Perseverance

My father passed away from the effects of rheumatoid arthritis in 2002. Moma took it hard but immediately returned to work after his funeral. Work and standing behind that chair always gave her peace and purpose.

Soon after, one customer's husband died, and mom told me her customer told her she was afraid at night. She said, "I told Thelma to get a book, say her prayers, read till she got really sleepy, and trust the good Lord to watch over her." Mom's trust in God and positive outlook was inspiring to so many. She was better than a counselor to her ladies, and most would cling to her advice. Her Southern charm and raw, unpretentious faith and boldness was endearing.

Another lady, Jackie, married for the second time after her husband of many years left her for another woman. Mom was thrilled for her when she met a nice man who seemingly adored her. They got married, but after a while, she told mom she was leaving him and getting herself an apartment. Mom told her she needed to work that out with him and be thankful she had a man living who loved her!

Every Monday on our outings, I'd hear the recap of her week. She truly loved her customers, and they were all her friends. She cared about their well-being.

Ruby was a unique woman whom Moma had as a customer when I was young. I remember hearing she once had a nervous breakdown. Moma felt sorry for her; she seemed lonely even though she was married and had two or three kids. She came every Saturday, and one Saturday I was at the salon with Moma, hanging out. I'm not sure where my dad was that day but probably playing golf. Ruby asked mom if I could go home with her, and Moma said yes to lift her spirit. She wanted me to see her doll collection and would fix my lunch. Let's just say it wasn't my cup of tea, and I never went back. But I look back, and it wasn't bad. Mom liked her even though she was very picky about her hair and hard to please. When she passed away mom was asked to fix her hair before her funeral. I remember Moma coming home after and saying she told Ruby, "All these years, we've done it your way; now we are doing it my way."

She could always find a way to make any situation lighter by saying something funny. I think she said that to keep from crying. The moral of the story is, we need all kinds of people to mold us, even the hard ones.

Daddy, B. W. Cook

Suitors

A few of her ladies had dementia, and I recall one of them continued to come until she passed away as her husband would bring her each week for her hairdo! Mom would always say how kind he was to his wife and say, "Poor old thing." She felt bad for him, knowing the end was inevitable. She, having already lost my daddy, knew what it would be like for him and was always compassionate.

The lady did pass away, and her husband continued to stop by the salon to see my mom. He would just want to say hi and check on her. At holidays, she'd mention he would bring her a box of chocolate or a flower. She would always tell me and preface it with "That poor thing (and his name) brought me candy. He is so nice." She said all the ladies she worked with told her he was pursuing her. She didn't want any part of that!

But finally, one afternoon he stopped by her salon and asked her if she'd go for coffee with him sometime.

Moma said, "I told him: I'm sorry, Jim; I can't. I'm not thirsty!" The ladies at the salon, she said, were in stitches laughing but trying to convince Moma to take him up on it. He was a good man. She told me, "I mean, I like him, and he's nice as can be, but your daddy would come unglued." She said, "Joyce, your daddy would come out of that grave if I even talked to anyone." Truth is, she didn't want anyone else besides Dad. In her mind, she and Dad were still married, and she was not going to go anywhere with another man! "That man was devoted to his wife and missed her terribly; poor thing is just lonesome," she'd say. I know Moma enjoyed knowing him and always spoke highly of his kindness. But in her understanding of marriage and commitment, it went all the way to heaven. No amount of theology would convince her otherwise.

When Moma passed away, I found her and Daddy's picture and one of just my daddy in her wallet. It made me smile. At her visitation, I saw an elderly man walking out of the funeral chapel. I hadn't spoken to him as I was engaged in conversation with someone else when I saw him pass by her coffin. I hurriedly ran up to introduce myself to the mysterious man. I recognized his name—Jim; it was the man who asked Moma to coffee. He said, "Your mother was a kind woman." I was touched that he came.

Sooner Rather Than Later

Looking back, what a meaningful time that was! If I ever wondered the impact of my moma, or a hairdresser, it was when she passed away from this earth. It was so apparent, the woman, the legend in her own way, was no longer present in our lives, and it was so surreal. How many times I'd heard my moma say "Well, they're better off" at the news of someone passing away. Of course, it was always someone who'd suffered a lengthy illness. But unlike them, she had always rallied and gotten better. Returning to her spunky, Sunday-cooking, Monday-shopping self.

One time, about ten years before her passing, she had gotten really sick. She made an appointment with the doctor, and he discovered a large mass in her abdomen near an ovary. He referred her immediately to a gynecologist and then on to a gynecological oncologist. It was concerning, and surgery was the next step to determine if the mass was malignant.

The morning of her surgery, we left for the hospital. Moma was briefing me. She was well into her eighties, and the surgeon had told her it could be risky just because of her advanced age. She informed me that if she didn't make it through surgery, she didn't want me to put her age in her obituary. I said, "First, Moma, you aren't going to die, but why can't I put your age?"

She said, "Joyce Ann, those women will come unglued if they know how old I am; promise me you'll not tell them."

"Of course," I said, "Ok, but you're crazy. You should be proud of your age and that you're still going strong!"

She said, "I am, but they might quit coming to me for their hair if they know. And another thing," she said. I asked what it was. "Don't go putting that I've gone to meet the Lord; that's a given! Everyone is gonna meet the Lord, and I hope they can tell I knew him already! I'll tell you one thing," she added, "some are gonna wish they'd met him sooner!"

I laughed and said, "Ok, Moma, I won't put that!"

Mondays

It seems Mondays have a bad rap with most people, but not hairdressers. At least not the old-school ones like my moma and me. Now it's changed, but way back when, all hair salons were closed on Mondays! Ever since I was born, it was mine and Moma's day. Before I was born, she spent it with my favorite aunt Margaret; then after I came, I went everywhere with them. And this kept on until two weeks before she passed from this earth to heaven. Sometimes one of my friends Debbie or Susan would go too.

Usually, it would entail a trip to the local beauty supply first to pick up the weeks' worth of colors and perms, then out to Northeast Mall in Hurst, Texas, to hit our favorite stores of the day, Casual Corner, Accessory Lady, The Limited, or JCPenney. We sometimes didn't buy a thing, but all the clerks knew us by name.

Then we'd end the afternoon with a great lunch. I mentioned the Accessory Lady, but it was actually at another smaller mall down the road from Northeast called North Hills Mall. Anyway, I always looked forward to Mondays, and Moma did too. She would often say, "I hope our Monday doesn't get loused up!" She meant anything that would keep us from being together. I used to think she was just kidding, but I know now as a mom any second with your kids is a treasured moment, no matter how or where. She knew time together and shopping were my love languages, and it was hers too.

Sometimes for a special occasion, we would head to West Fort Worth to Ridgmar Mall. Back then, it was the hoity-toity shopping Mecca of Fort Worth! Besides Neiman Marcus, there were a few other nice trendy shops and restaurants there, El Fenix, and Chelsea Street Pub. When my aunt Margaret was with us, we would eat at El Fenix. Wherever we went, it was a real treat and fun time.

We would always go there for a special occasion like a birthday, or when we needed Estée Lauder perfume, even though I'm pretty sure you could buy that perfume at Dillard's in Northeast Mall. Anyway, we really went just to eat at Neiman Marcus's delicious Hedges Tea Room. We loved to get the hot popovers and strawberry butter and that little cup of broth. We would always dress a little better going over there to fit in with the upscale West Fort Worth patrons we'd often see.

It was a cold Monday, and Moma decided to wear her new faux-fur vest she'd bought at Accessory Lady for

$39.99 on a previous shopping day. She looked so pretty in the vest, and I know she felt fancy; she definitely looked the part. As we finished and we walked out of the tea room, a lady approached her and said, "Excuse me, your fur vest is lovely; where might I ask did you get it?"

Moma didn't miss a beat and said, "Oh honey, thank you; I got it at Koslows!" I almost choked on my chocolate mint! The lady thanked her, and Moma and I laughed all the way out of Neiman Marcus.

I said, "Moma, you know you didn't get it at Koslows!"

She said, "Joyce Ann, that woman probably hasn't ever heard of Accessory Lady. I surely didn't want to confuse her." Oh my, she always kept me laughing!

Moma and Aunt Margaret

Moma shopping on Mondays

Mondays continued but our destinations changed. The mall became too much walking for her with her knee pain, but we continued to spend almost every Monday together.

One Monday, she had an appointment with a new knee doctor in Fort Worth. He'd been highly recommended by one of her friends as the best. As we entered the room, pictures adorned his room with all the magazine covers of his pictures as Top Doc, Best Doctor, and so on. He walked in and introduced himself to Mom and me. She then said, "Well, I hope you're what they say you are, but have you ever seen a knee as ugly and worn out as mine?" He laughed and assured her he had.

Those memories of our times together are some of my most cherished ones.

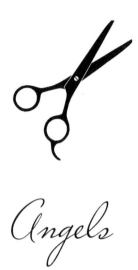

Angels

The last time my moma and I had our usual "Monday with Moma" time we spent out together, unbeknownst to us, the next couple of weeks would look drastically different. That Monday like most Mondays, we headed out for a usual day together.

We made a trip to the Target by my house to get cat food and her essentials and had lunch at one of our favorite places, Cotton Patch. She loved the chicken-fried steak, black-eyed peas, and rolls. It was consistently good and tender. We finished right around noon as we always ate an early lunch. As we left the restaurant, I helped her out to my car as she wanted to walk with me. Sometimes, I would run to get the car and pull up close to her, but that day she wanted to walk. She also had her cane. As we slowly headed to my car, a brand-new white pickup truck slowed down and stopped in the busy crossway from the restaurant to the parking lot. I saw a man, and he rolled his window down and said something, but I couldn't hear him. He then put his truck in park, got out of it, and walked over to us. He was around thirty or so and looked very nice. He came up to my moma and said, "Excuse me, I just want to hug you and tell you what a blessing I know you are to everyone. I lost my grandmother a month ago and seeing you reminded me of her." Then he hugged us both, said "God bless you," got in his truck, and drove away. He waved at the cars he had momentarily stopped while making this kind gesture to her. My moma was shocked, amazed, and very touched, and so was I. We talked about it all the way back to her house, and I recall her saying bless his heart.

I feel like she was literally touched by an angel that day, and it was as if God affirmed her in every way through a stranger. The words he spoke were more than true. She always had such a servant's heart and loved us all so well. She would give you the shirt off her back and expect nothing in return. After she hurt her back and had to stop working at ninety-two years old, I begged her to let us throw her a retirement party, and she said "absolutely not, I'm not sure I'm retiring!"

We had no idea that God would be calling her home in just a few weeks from that day at Cotton Patch. I can tell you that it's not something I ever thought of. I couldn't bear the thought of it. I know that no one in our entire family could either.

I just wanted to share the story of that last outing my moma and I had. It's been almost four years; sometimes

I'm ok, and sometimes I'm not. It's hard and different without her, and I don't like it. My sweet counselor friend told me that was ok! I think sometimes people think that you must be strong if you are a person of faith, and that is not true.

Moma worked with many other stylists over her years in the Salon! So many of them were very special to her; like mine are and have been to me. You become like family in this business and especially in an open-concept salon setting like she always had. The first was Suella, who was awesome in every way. She and Mom knew each other so well and were around the same age. Moma and Suella had quite the bond.

I remember the day of Suella's funeral. Mom said, "Joyce, I'm so upset; I don't want to go." We went, and midway through, she whispered to me, "Joyce Ann, we have got to go. I can't stay; I must get to that beauty shop. Suella's known me, and she would understand; come on!" Before I could stop her, she walked up to the front of the church and told Suella's husband, and we left. I am sure they understood and undoubtedly knew Mom adored her and so did I!

Sandra

At the end of Mom's career, there was Sandra! She was younger than Mom, and I can't begin to tell you how proud Mom was of her! I would worry myself sick, thinking about my ninety-year-old mother trying to get into the salon with her arthritic knees. Moma would say, "Joyce Ann, now don't you worry about me; Sandra watches me like a hawk! She won't let anyone bother me or anything happen to me if she can help it!" So, I put her number in my phone, and one day it rang; her number came up on the screen.

It was a Saturday, and I knew Moma was working! I answered and Sandra said, "Joyce Ann, your mom had a car accident as she left the salon. I saw it and went right over; she's ok, but her car is banged up badly." Needless to say, I was shaken! I called my oldest brother, Welton, as he lived closer, and he went over to assess the situation. We were so grateful that Sandra was able to be with our moma that day. I know it shook her more than she let on. That day and all the days ahead, I knew Sandra cared about Moma as much as Moma did about her. Thank you, Sandra, for being like her second pair of hands those last years! She loved, cared for, and was prouder of you... more than you know.

Moma was really upset about this car accident. She was however determined to get another car. She insisted it was not her fault and that she had to get back behind the wheel as soon as possible. My brothers and I tried to put it off as long as possible, but she even cornered my husband Russell to see if he thought we should find her a car. She asked him one Sunday afternoon, in front of all of us, didn't he think that if she could write a check and pay for it, shouldn't we take her to buy a car! She didn't want to depend on anyone to take her to work at the beauty shop! Well, off we went on a Monday, and she did buy herself a car at ninety-one!

Moma and Sandra

Moma at ninety-one with her new car

The Giver

I've never known anyone with a servant heart quite like my moma. She was truly that to anyone, no matter if they needed it or not. Sometimes it wasn't in a monetary way; sometimes it was just in the way she treated people. Usually though, it was what she could do for them. Also, it didn't matter if they could afford it or not. She didn't care; she just was here to serve others, and she did it better than just about anyone I've ever seen.

We would often be shopping, and she would say, "Joyce Ann, I need to get a cross bracelet like the one I have for (fill in a name—whoever). She just loved mine, and I want to surprise her with one." Sometimes it was her favorite scent at Bath & Body Works—Japanese Cherry Blossom. She would have to buy one of her customers a body lotion. Or we would be at Target, and she would buy a certain type of granola bar, candy, cracker, or something for her customers. She loved to give them something to snack on while they were under the hair dryer. She would also tell me how some loved just how she fixed their coffee for them. She did it all without complaining. She absolutely found joy in serving and blessing others. This was always her, and when I was growing up, she wouldn't just buy me something; if one of my friends went along, they got something too. On most Sundays, we would all go to Moma's for lunch.

She would take great delight in fixing special things for lunch on Sundays, especially for the grandsons Brian, Travis, Erik, Ethan, and Evan. Like roast, pinto beans, and her amazing corn bread. You name it. She wanted everyone to feel like VIPs. This wasn't exclusive to just family; she loved making a big pot of pinto beans and her corn bread for the beauty shop ladies too!

I think her giving nature was from a heart filled with so much gratitude to God that she wanted to bless others. She would often tell me, "You can't outgive the good Lord."

Her family were farmers, and I think my grandfather may have also worked in a factory; they had very little growing up. But she would say her family and their strong ties and faith was all she needed. They were all so close, even her cousins. They called her "Shug," short for Sugar. She lived up to it too as her tea was the sweetest in Texas! When she told my grandparents she was going to beauty school, my grandfather told her she'd always have a job because no matter how bad the economy was, ladies would always want to look pretty! Moma always liked to see pretty people, so I think she picked the right profession!

Magnetism

Customers will gravitate to you; some stay and some don't. I knew most of my mom's customers, at the very least by their names! Hardly ever did I hear of one whom I didn't hear of for years and years. They all seemed to adore Mom, and she adored them too! Up until close to the end of her career, she was still getting calls from ladies who'd ask if she'd take them on as clients.

One lady was trying to get on her appointment book, and Moma was informed by the salon owner that she wasn't allowed to come there. Mom asked why, and the owner said she owed her money for a perm and had refused to pay. Moma found out the lady had dementia; a couple of Mom's customers knew the lady and told her. Assuming that it was the cause of why the lady hadn't paid, Moma let the owner know of the lady's situation and asked her, "How much does she owe you?" She then wrote her a check for seventy-five dollars. She said,

"Joyce, that poor lady has to get her hair done; I just have to take her even if I had to pay for that perm she owed." She loved her customers; of course, she had some who were more special than others, but it was the shorter of the list. Still, she was dedicated to them till the very end of her career at ninety-one years of age!

Even up to the day before she went into the hospital, which unbeknownst to us would be one of her last days at home, she was calling one of her hairdresser friends to make an appointment for one of her former customers. I recall saying, "Moma, she can call her; just give her the number." But she did it anyway, always putting others before herself.

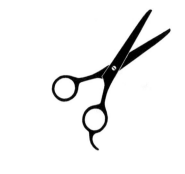

Fresh Starts

Faith and prayer were essential in my moma's life, as was church too. She attended regularly, every Sunday but usually not special ladies' events. She had work on Saturdays, and she did not like to drive in the evening. A few years after my dad had passed, Mom told me it was really getting depressing going to church. I said, "What do you mean?"

She told me that all her friends there were dying off. She said, "It's down to me and Pauline, and she's not here for long either." She also said it was just lonesome looking at that sanctuary and thinking about Daddy and remembering him walking down that aisle with the offering plate and not seeing him do that anymore made her lonesome. I told her to look for another church, but she said, "I really can't. I'll just tough it out."

Not long after, the church announced they were relocating to Bedford, Texas. A gentleman from church named Buster called offering to caravan with the older members, guiding them to the new location. Mom told me, "I appreciate his offer, but I'm not going to Bedford with Buster." She said, "I'll now have to go somewhere else close to home," and she did. I know it was good for her, and she loved it!

Fern and Earline

Saying the right people will gravitate to you is a fact, and I know myself, as a stylist and growing up in a salon, that your clientele is going to do that.

Moma had a customer named Fern; she was a beautiful soul and full of faith! You would have thought she was Billy Graham if you could have heard Mom speak of her! Moma thought her prayers went higher than anyone, so she would always have Fern pray for whatever she felt was an urgent need. I have no doubt Fern had prayed countless prayers for our family along with Mom and Suella. After I graduated and went to work at The Nut Shell with Mom, I witnessed the strong ties of faith between all of them. I do not know if they had a clue what an example they all were to me, but I wish I could tell them. My heart is grateful, nonetheless.

Another customer, Earline, was a key member in Mom's customer base. She was an RN. Besides giving

Mom her B12 shots, one evening it was quite the blessing she was at the beauty shop for her weekly appointment. Moma wore glasses, and it had been a long day at the salon. Sometimes beauty supply salesmen would leave samples of something on her station. Earline was under the dryer, and mom removed her glasses and mistakenly picked up a bottle of nail-polish remover for eye drops. She poured it in her eye by accident! I was a teenager and remember Dad getting the call that Earline immediately flushed Mom's eye with water and drove her to the new emergency clinic that had recently opened in the neighborhood! Earline really saved Mom's eye, and she was so grateful to her.

The next six weeks, mom worked with a patch over that eye, but in true Wilma fashion, she never missed a day of work. Crazy enough, she did not seem near as fazed by what had happened and the near damage of her eye at all. She was more impressed with the new satellite emergency medical center in the neighborhood and Earline's quick nursing skills.

Moma and Earline

Excerpts from My Journal: Seeking

Today I went for a long walk. Lately my physical fitness has been sidelined, and I need to get back at it! I sometimes listen to books, podcasts, or my Pandora radio, but today I didn't even have the mental energy to look for anything. I lost my mom two weeks ago today, November 14, to a sudden illness. If you know me and Mom, you know how close we were. I talked to her two times a day and saw her every week, spending every Monday with her and many Sundays too!

We could talk about anything, and sometimes we'd even be thinking the same thing. To say I miss her would be an understatement. Anyway, as I was walking and thinking about the last few weeks and mom, I discovered that in some ways, I almost feel closer to her than ever. I asked God why and how, and it occurred to me it's because I've been seeking ways to know and feel her presence more than ever. Not that I wouldn't when she was alive and well but not all the time.

I realized that it's the same with God!

Oh, I do that sometimes but not always. I recalled the scripture in Jeremiah 29:13: "You will seek me; you will find me if you seek me with all your heart!"

That brings us so much hope. It follows one of my favorite verses Jeremiah 29:11: "'For I know the plans I have for you,' declares the LORD, 'plans to prosper you and not to harm you, plans to give you hope and a future.'"

I saw my mom draw closer and closer to God after my dad passed away until she passed. She was doing this same thing, I realized, seeking. Now her faith has been made sight!

We will all pass away; what are we seeking? The kingdom of heaven never passes! I'm so blessed to know that my mom, dad, and many loved ones are there in heaven with Jesus!

Feeling thankful for the message God gave me today that he is with us! If you feel alone, seek him!

God Winks and Heavenly Appointments

One day a couple of years after Moma passed away, I got a phone call from a lady I didn't know named Betty. She'd gotten my number from a lady who knew me and asked if I could take her on an upcoming Thursday for a shampoo and set. She said she had to have it rolled in rollers and teased or it would stay in. Her grandson was getting married, and her regular stylist was on vacation. She said, "I heard you might be able to set my hair." I thought about it, and even though I truthfully don't like doing that, I told her I would take her.

That day she came in the salon and handed me a picture. It was an older photograph of her and her husband from a cruise they'd taken years back. She told me that it was how she liked her hair combed, and she had to have lots of back-combing and hair spray. The picture told me that, and I was silently praying that I could pull it off.

We began getting acquainted, and I soon found out that she had lived at one time in the area of Fort Worth where I grew up. She then went on to say that in fact the hairstylist she had gone to for years before she moved to Keller had done her hair in that picture. I asked her who that was, thinking maybe I knew her having lived over in that neck of the woods. She then said, "Her name was Wilma." I looked at her, tears welling in my eyes, and then she said "Wait; are you Joyce Ann, her daughter?"

I said, "Yes!"

She was as happy as I was and then went on to tell me how much she loved Moma, how she couldn't wait to tell her husband when he picked her up, and how she loved the way my moma always did her hair. She asked me about my boys, my brothers, and my nephews, knowing all kinds of details about our lives. My heart was so happy and thankful that I had said yes to something I normally would have said no to. I almost missed a huge blessing. I couldn't wait till I could call Russell and tell him. I called friends to tell them too. Brenda said that was a God wink. I know my moma and Suella were smiling and sending love all the way from heaven.

An appointment heaven sent

Epilogue

Mom and I were so close. I thought by now, almost four years later, I would be more used to her being gone. The sun still rises and shines, but I feel as if there is a cloud in my soul that has dimmed my spirit! I am better if I stay busy and keep my calendar full of activity! Thankfully, that is not hard for me to do! But through it all, I know that God is good, and I have even felt thankful that Moma was not subjected to the pandemic of 2020–2021, or even the tumultuous, crazy political climate we live in. It goes without saying, I miss her like crazy, especially on Mondays and our morning and evening phone calls!

The hope I have without her presence with us is to cling to my faith, my husband Russell, my boys, and all the precious family, friends, and customers I am blessed with! In closing, I want to say thank you for the memories, Moma, and for instilling in me a strong work ethic! She never would give up or say she retired even when she did! She would not hear of having a retirement party because she would say, "I might go back sometime!" She said this at ninety-one; that was just how she was. So, think of this memoir as her retirement party to celebrate her and the career she loved. I love it too and am so blessed to be where I stand. I love you, Moma!

CPSIA information can be obtained
at www.ICGtesting.com
Printed in the USA
BVHW052047050123
655447BV00035B/206